CW00427877

The following pages contain poems featured in a live show that began as a performance at The MET Theatre in Kansas City, USA, in the Summer of 2016.

More poems were written and in May and August 2017, these formed a full-length show performed in Brighton, then Edinburgh, UK, respectively under the title "Slooshy Wordshow." The word "slooshy" is in fact taken from 'A Clockwork Orange' by Anthony Burgess, being part of the 'nadsat' slang used by the characters in the novel – it means 'to hear, to listen'.

Dropping the word "slooshy" and substituting some material for newer works, the show in this modified form then went to Adelaide, Australia in March 2018 simply as "Wordshow".

GREG BYRON is the performance persona of Gavin Robertson, who has a long ongoing career as a theatre-deviser, Performer, Writer and Director. There seems to be a degree of confusion over whether performing poetry is 'Spoken Word', 'Performance Poetry' or 'Live Literature' – and in the end it probably doesn't matter very much. The poems in this collection are, in Greg's own words "probably better as something heard – with all the resonance and inflections of the human voice – than read off the page"... but, as you're reading this, it's probably too late now! That's the difference between performance and simply reading the words.

Hopefully, you'll enjoy the tone and occasional bite of the poems, and perhaps if you're reading them having seen a live show, it'll bring back the memory of that event.

You can keep up with new material, live shows and general information at the website – www.gregbyron.co.uk

... and you can also follow Greg as he drops his thoughts and observations on Twitter, using the moniker @gregbyronwords

Feel free to pass the words around...

All photos: Mark Dimmock

IF YOU'RE NOT ANGRY- ARE YOU AWAKE?

If you're not Angry, are you awake?

Are you off social media, just for the sake

Of your sanity. It's vanity - as we all know

I'm as guilty as you are of wanting to show

That my life is thrilling, exciting and sunny

Pictures of airports and selfies and funny
friends doing photobombs, laughing and well.

It's the everyday highlife we all want to sell.

Every tweet tweeting 'happy', and 'busy' and
'yes'

'Cos narcissm helps us avoid the mess that the
world's in around us with no sign of stopping

And even then signs want to upset your
shopping-

"Thanks for your gifts of food and support"

As we leave stony-faced with the goods we
just bought

I'm angry a sign just offered me thanks

It's two zero - something-what's fine about
foodbanks!?

If you're not angry, are you awake?

Disability cuts "we are all Daniel Blake!"

A trumped-up US leader, campaigns that were fake –

Never mind - save something for that rainy day

But not 'til you're 70 (thanks Theresa May)

Raise the age of retirement, buy Trident, kick butts

But tell us you still need austerity cuts.

My son's still at home, probably will be at thirty

But tell me again how the poor are just dirty

Cheaters and layabouts, quote me the facts

Convince me while I shell out for your bedroom tax.

There isn't a plan, but we'll be alt-right

As they come for us all in't middle of t' night

"We've just got some questions, you'll come to no harm"

God bless Orwell and Animal Farm.

History repeats and it's not like we're blind

But we can't seem to stop it so one day we'll find

That if Guy Fawkes, Wat Tyler and Ghandi are dead –

There's no-one but us to start leading instead.

I don't know what's coming, my chances I'll take-

But if YOU'RE not angry, are you awake?

ORANGE WAS NOT THE ONLY FRUIT

Orange was not the only fruit

But don't let a Woman – first lady to boot,

Into your White House, she's small and she's frail

She might have been nasty- we've looked at her email.

How can <u>she</u> make the US great again

You need business sense and acumen

We don't know what came from behind th'iron curtain

But there's no more 'United' States' either, that's certain,

When health sparks revolt, just cancer reflected

Your twitter feed shows who the US elected

As the downtrodden feel the sharp end of his boot

Cry out Orange. Was. Not. The. Only. Fruit.

MAGIC MONEY TREE

Theresa May's found a magic money tree

Growing in her garden for the DUP

Picked a billion leaves with her magic green fingers

To hand out freely to the Irish right wingers

But left two upright so that we could see

How she applies the rules of austerity -

Expendable in politics but not for you and me.

Theresa May's found a magic money tree

Kept it in the shade of hypocrisy

Shook its silver branches for majority

Watered it with words so it grew up strong and stable

Shored up with corpses of the ill and disabled

It won't shed leaves for the poor or NHS

It only drops its fruit when Theresa whispers 'Yes'...

REALITY TV

Reality... reality TV for the masses

A Rolls Royce with no chassis

A ship launched on molasses

The Bolshoi on their asses

All hot air and gases

Like specs without glasses

Spectacle, freak show, talent contest,
desperation without discerning

A modern-day Barnum's circus earning

At the expense of dignity or discernment.

"There's a sucker born every minute"

Reality? We're all in it!

ADVICE TO MY 16-YEAR OLD SELF

Don't be in awe of older people. They're old
not wise

You've got exams - so revise

Look a girl in the eyes

Don't worry about size

Everyone lies.

Learn to play slap bass

Remember Grandad's face

Spend more time at his place.

'Cos... everyone dies.

Don't be such a gent

Make bold your intent

Your girlfriend's got hormones just like you

Dare to do what you'd like to

Cos she'd like it too!

No-one else in the world is as unique as you.

Don't try to fit in

Don't go babysittin'

Don't drive before you've passed your test

Don't cheek the police when he tests your breath

Don't be sulky in front of the magistrate

Tell your parents you love 'em before it's too late.

Don't be a New Romantic - you're not Duran Duran

Don't form that band!

Don't be an also-ran

Do the best you can. Have a career plan!

Don't fret over acne- I promise it'll pass

Don't be scared of a lass

Don't be intimidated by class.

Practice peace of mind, be kind.

Never mind - If you're not on telly

If you don't write like Shelly

If your legs are like jelly

When you ask a girl out

If you don't ask – there's nowt.

Don't be so shy

Don't be afraid to ask 'why'

Don't lie.

Don't be too polite to put yourself first

Bounce back when your bubble's burst

Don't be coerced

Dive in headfirst – but pick the right time

Don't spend hours looking for the perfect rhyme.

Don't be material,

Say "goodbye" to Imperial...

Eat more cereal

Eat less fried

Choose in whom you confide

Go along for the ride

Be impulsive, be daring

Worry less what you're wearing

Enjoy life- don't get disenchanted

And don't take a full head of hair for granted.

SUFFER THE CHILDREN

"I wandered lonely as a cloud

That floats on high o'er vales and hills..."

When all at once I saw a crowd

A bird's eye view –through the blue, no frills....

A child, tears still flowing as she waited at Calais

As the police destroyed her makeshift tent and sent her on her way...

And next to her, another girl, a truant for the week

Not having funds for tampons stays away from school while bleak,

And hollow-eyed, her mother stands beside her on the hill

Saying nothing, so that's what she gets, despite her being ill.

And as I watch 4-million kids converge upon the mount

The number in child poverty – at least, at the last count.

That's one-in-four to make it clear in terms we understand

The poor created by the laws we have across the land.

They've all got names as well of course, they're not just handy figures

But if you live in poverty, you're one of the Tories' niggers

'Cos you're lazy and you're dirty and you should be out at work

You just had kids to get a council house but that won't work

'Cos we don't invest in social housing- we let market forces

Determine what gets built and sold – it's horses for our courses...

So listen Sarah, Sally, Tim, Terry, Jo and Bobby

Becky, Jack, John at the back, and little brother Robbie,

Ben and Billy, Skye and Tilly, Poppy and Edwina

Clutching sister Mia's skirts, you think I hadn't seen her?

Well things could be much worse you know, young lady at the back...

You could be from Afghanistan, or Syria or Iraq

Stuck in the Calais Jungle unaccompanied, alone

A refugee, you see, you flee - and end up with no home.

Unless our Dubs Amendment got you over here and settled

Just 200 not 3000 like we promised, which has nettled

The electorate apparently.

We're not a charity

So excuse the polarity, between humanitarian action

And selling arms to a faction one of whom we support while the other gets nought.

So – Amira, Ameena, Mohammed and Joram,

Rosarita, little Sara, brother Ahmed and Houmam,

You'll have to wait your turn - We've got 4-million here bereft

And after bailing out the banks, we'll have to see what's left.

FIBONACCI:

1, 1, 2, 3, 5, 8, thirteen

Fibonacci's sequence, nature's pristine

Arrangement gives order to chaos – unseen.

Every number's the total of the previous two

Plants don't know the sequence - yet the ratio's true

For their survival – ours too.

Called the Golden Ratio, the Greek letter Phi

Our esteem for beauty is directed by

1.618 relating to the human eye.

The length of arm, the human face,

The human hand, each bone in place

The fingers, profile and each toe

Conform to the Golden Ratio.

Our four front teeth, the whites of your eyes

Your ankle to thigh, your credit card size,

The length of Spock's ears AND the Starship Enterprise.

The art of Da Vinci - The Mona Lisa

The pyramid at Giza, the Tower at Pisa

Where Fibonacci was born- now there's a teaser...

The bracts of a pinecone, florets of a flower,

There's no art without mathematical power.

Everything's connected – art, science and reason

A snapshot of God can be seen in a season,

A fossil, the seeds in an apple

Or maybe it's bollocks and this is a raffle –

1, 1, 2, 3, 5, 8 thirteen...

And on to infinity numbers unseen

Ratios, rectangles, patterns and flow...

21, 34 – onwards we go

55, 89, one four four

In our 1.618, foot to the floor

Faster and faster and faster we go

As the years gain momentum, 'til one day we know

What the whole point was, the rhyme and the reason

Unless there's no God. At the last – in conclusion

Patterns and order amongst the confusion

Let us glimpse worlds in a grain of white sand

Hold infinity in the palm of your 1.6 hand.

AN IRON BAR IS MOSTLY EMPTY SPACE

An iron bar is mostly empty 'space- the final frontier'

Jumbled meanings mask the truth – what's really happening here?

As NASA's senior rover slowly crawls on the Red Planet

Scientists and analysts pore over what began it.

Is there Life on Mars they say or could there ever have 'bin'

Conspiracies and thoughts like these from Ibetha to King's Lynn

Confound the working man and woman struggling to stay warm

The cold and empty void of space seems hardly to conform

To any kind of problem that they're having to contend

With.

They're trying to keep going, to control the nitty-gritty

The irony in naming Mars' new rover 'Opportunity'

Lost on them as Earthbound values seem to bend and waver

Austerity, authority where cuts are the new flavour

Replacing care, compassion - out of fashion and decreasing –

What the hell has space to do with levels of policing

And private means and cronyism, health and income tax

Give us here a better world and keep your NASA facts.

We don't believe you ever went- there's buildings on the moon

Or are the photos doctored –photoshopped by some buffoon?

We don't believe you anymore, we don't believe in ET

Give us something with some weight, give us something meaty

Give us solar heating if you want to harness space

Replace the coal with wind, in fact look up the word 'replace'

Analyse alternatives for here not outer space.

Knowledge is all very well, the search for information

But knowing just for knowing's sake is hardly conservation

We can't know where we're going if we never look behind

You have to join the dots to make a brand new dotted line.

An iron bar is mostly empty space- that's pretty trite

When gazing at the stars we see the depths of endless night

Too aware of Climate change and death to stay polite

Rage, rage against the dying of <u>our</u> light.

Article 50

So she triggered the transition

Took the 'Great' from our Great Britain

Though the ink with which it's written isn't dry.

Hand delivered it to Brussels flexing nationalistic muscles

With a pasty plan that's all pie-in-the-sky.

Still maybe I shouldn't fuss

'Cos according to a bus

There's a good few million for the NHS.

Though a paltry one percent

For the nurses' pay won't dent

The expenses nor the underfunded mess.

But with all of the conjecture

There's still room to hear a lecture

On how opportunities will come our way

Though the pound is on the ground

I can roundly hear the sound

Of the Tories all applauding Theresa May.

First lady unelected

Which one of us suspected

That the U would be stripped from the U of K?

And despite applause or booing

We've got other troubles brewing

They say every dog will surely have its day...

For the Scots want Indy 2

And this time it might come true

They seem open to what Nicola might say.

So here's to me and you

Red, white and feeling blue...

I'll be seeing you, Theresa

If I can get a visa

I'll head off to France or Spain

Be in Europe again.

Though my pound will buy me zip

It'll still be worth the trip

And I'll turn and look back

At the Union Jack

All fluttery and wavy

At the mast of the ENGLISH navy.

Time to draw a breath and wait- Great Brexit's in our future

You can change your mind if isolation doesn't suit yer -

They say that it's reversible

So if in your submersible

That bloody great baby

In the bathwater maybe

Seems suddenly daft

You can hop on a raft

'Cos it's not a done deal

You can always appeal

To the UK that's left

And politically bereft.

Well - here's to your legacy – an island lost and lean

God save our fucking futures and God save the fucking Queen.

AN OLD MAN SPEAKS THE BLUES

A friend and I were talking, sat sipping tea one day

As through the murky window-pane, the sky hung low and grey

The liquid, scalding hot and strong, suggested 'life's OK'

A barricade against the rain that chased the sun away.

The Radio was gently playing Fleetwood Mac's 'The Chain'

I hopped up to turn the volume down, then sat back down again.

"I'm 82 next week" announced my friend behind his china

As biscuits crumbs cascaded on a rug that had seen finer days.

"I worked from leaving school and retired at fifty-five,

The day I stopped commuting was the day I came alive.

I never had a fortune but I holidayed abroad

I borrowed here and there but always what I could afford.

And never missed a payment, no, nor drank nor gambled neither

I kept the house in fair condition, slipped me son a fiver

When I could, then added grandkids 2 and 3 and 4

Used the NHS just once when hipbone met the floor

Last year, but I came home when I was able"

He gestured to a paper lying face down on the table...

"That's the Lego Magazine- I get it here for Kelly

She's nearly six, it keeps her asking me what's on the telly...

And Will, he's eight in May, I asked him if he had a clue

For what he'd do when all grown-up, like all grandparents do

He wants a superpower – but one that's all his own

He says he'll be invisible, but only when alone

That cracked me up, it really did. Kids, they're really funny

Oh - and Kate says she'll teach other kids and be just like her Mummy.

I know" he said, "why Will and Kate! What were their parents thinking"...

He paused and filled the cup again before resuming drinking.

Beneath us on the radio, a song from 'Mama Mia'

Said 'thank you for the music' as the sky began to clear.

"I'm 82 next week" he said again, with added steel

"I'm not a bore about the war, but I know what I feel.

I can use a laptop, I've a mobile by the bed

I don't do tweets or Facebook, no - I've got a life instead.

Physically I'm telling you that getting older sucks

But on the other hand I couldn't give as many fucks

About what others think. You really start to know what's what

To worry less in general and appreciate what you've got.

When I was growing up I only had modest ambition

A house, a job, a woman who loved me, that was my mission

My free degree in engineering got us what is ours

My son's on interest-only, and his wife's on zero hours

Their kids will pay for a degree, they'll be no NHS

The way I see it we here in the West are in a mess.

Don't worry I'm not going to sit right here pontificating

The tea is getting colder and I've half a biscuit waiting."

When tea was cleared, he slowly steered his way to the front door

"Lock up on your way out" he said as rain began to pour

"Bloody Britain" he yelled cheerily as drops they fell like tears

And Bowie sang 'Run for the shadows in these Golden Years'.

35660757R00020

Printed in Great Britain
by Amazon